Goodman's Five-Star
ACTIVITY BOOKS

Test-Taker Practice Series

LEVEL A

Burton Goodman

JAMESTOWN PUBLISHERS

a division of NTC/CONTEMPORARY PUBLISHING GROUP
Lincolnwood, Illinois USA

Acknowledgments

Stories, articles, adaptations, and other instructional materials by Burton Goodman.
The author wishes to express profound gratitude to Matthew Goodman for his invaluable
assistance.

Cover Design
    Karen Christoffersen
Interior Illustrations
    Other Brother Design

ISBN: 0-8092-0445-2
Published by Jamestown Publishers,
a division of NTC/Contemporary Publishing Group, Inc.,
4255 West Touhy Avenue,
Lincolnwood (Chicago), Illinois, 60712-1975, U.S.A.
© 2001 by Burton Goodman
00 01 02 03 04 MN 10 9 8 7 6 5 4 3 2 1

CONTENTS

About the Series   4

Two Good Friends   6
a short story

Ride, Sally Ride   14
a true story

A Trip to The Gambia   22
a true story

The Room   32
a short story

The Life of the Rain Forest   40
a true story

Belling the Cat   48
a fable

A Zoo of Fish   56
a true story

Test-Taker Score Chart   Inside back cover

ABOUT THE SERIES

Goodman's Five-Star Activity Books, Level A reinforces and extends the exercises and literary themes in *Travels* and *More Travels* in *Goodman's Five-Star Stories,* Level A. This activity book can be used in conjunction with *Travels* and *More Travels,* or it can be used on a completely independent basis.

Goodman's Five-Star Activity Books
Test-Taker Practice Series

The *Goodman's Five-Star Activity Books* series has been specially designed to help students master the kinds of exercises most frequently found on standardized tests. The series uses high-quality multicultural nonfiction and fiction materials to familiarize students with the kinds of questions they are likely to encounter. At the same time, the books offer students numerous opportunities to improve their language arts skills and their test scores through practice.

Each book in the series focuses on developing skills and competencies in reading comprehension, mechanics, and writing. Provision is also made for study skills practice.

The **Reading Skills** section provides students with 10 standardized questions with an emphasis on critical thinking and vocabulary. The **Mechanics** section offers repeated practice in capitalization, punctuation, the comma, spelling, and grammar. The **Writing** section requires students to respond to a wide variety of specific and open-ended writing tasks.

The series includes a practical Test-Taker self-scoring feature that enables students to score and record their results.

Used along with the books in *Goodman's Five-Star Stories*, or on an independent basis, I feel certain that the *Goodman's Five-Star Activity Books* will help students develop the confidence and competency to improve their test scores. In addition, the books will help readers master many of the essential language arts skills they need for success in school and in life.

Burton Goodman

Two Good Friends

Pedro and Hector were friends. They had been friends for a long time. They did many things together.

One day they were walking through the woods. They were on their way to a lake. They planned to fish there.

They talked as they walked. Hector said, "We are good friends. Isn't that so?"

"Oh, yes," Pedro said. "We are very good friends."

Hector said, "I will tell you a story about two friends."

"All right," Pedro said.

This is the story that Hector told:

Two friends were walking down a road. One of the men saw an ax. It was a very good one. He could cut down big trees with that ax.

For additional exercises and theme-related stories about friends, see "Work Well Done" in *Travels* and "The Game" in *More Travels* in *Goodman's Five-Star Stories,* Level A.

The man bent down. He picked up the ax. Then he told his friend, "Look, I have found an ax."

The other man said, "You mean *we*. *We* have found an ax. We were walking together. We are good friends. We should share the ax. It should belong to *us*."

"Oh, no," said the other man. "*I* saw the ax first. It is mine . . . all mine."

The two men kept on walking. Just then a man came rushing toward them. He was very big. He looked very strong.

The man looked very, very angry. The friends could tell that the ax belonged to him.

"Oh, oh," said the man who was holding the ax. "We are in trouble now. What should we do?"

"*We?*" said the other man. "What do you mean *we*? Don't you remember what you said? The ax is not *ours*. It is *yours . . . all yours*. You would not share the ax. So why should I share the danger? Goodbye!"

Pedro and Hector laughed.

"That could never happen to us," Hector said.

Just then the two boys saw a bear. The bear was very big. It began to run straight at them.

Not far from the boys was a tree. Hector was tall and thin. He could run very fast. He quickly ran to the tree. He reached up to a branch. Hector pulled himself up into the tree.

Pedro ran to the tree. He reached up, but he was too short. He could not reach the branch.

"Help me!" called Pedro to his friend. "Help me up into the tree! Pull me up! Pull me up!"

Hector was afraid. He feared the bear very much. He began to climb. He climbed higher and higher. He climbed all the way up to the top of the tree.

Pedro did not know what to do. The huge bear was coming closer and closer. Pedro threw himself down on the ground. He lay very still. He did not move at all. Pedro made believe he was dead.

The bear walked up to Pedro. It put its nose against Pedro's head. The bear smelled Pedro. It thought that Pedro was dead.

Bears do not touch dead meat. So the bear walked away.

Hector waited for a little while. Then he came down from the tree. He walked over to Pedro.

"Pedro!" Hector said. "I was watching from the tree. I saw what happened. I saw the bear bend over you. It put its mouth next to your ear. What did the bear say?"

Pedro looked at Hector. Then Pedro said, "The bear whispered to me, 'The boy in the tree is not your friend. He will not help you when you need him.'"

I. Reading Skills

Fill in the circle next to the right answer.

1. This story is mostly about
   - (A) bears.
   - (B) trees.
   - (C) fishing.
   - (D) friends.

2. Which words belong in Box 1?
   - (A) could not run fast
   - (B) climbed to the top of a tree
   - (C) threw himself on the ground
   - (D) was not afraid of the bear

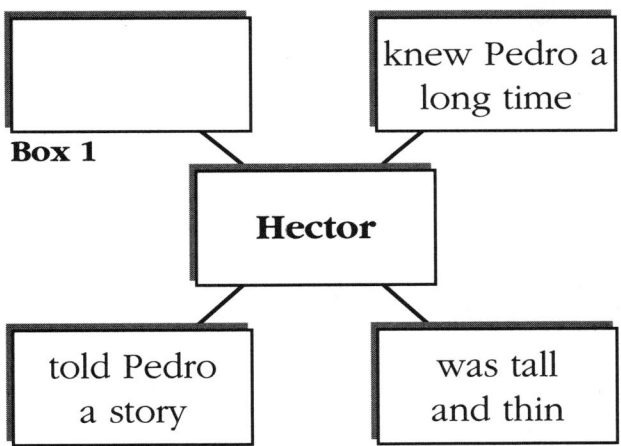

Box 1

knew Pedro a long time

Hector

told Pedro a story

was tall and thin

3. The man who lost the ax was
   - (A) kind.
   - (B) short.
   - (C) angry.
   - (D) weak.

4. The man who found the ax thought it should be his because he
   - (A) lost it.
   - (B) needed it very much.
   - (C) saw it first.
   - (D) planned to give it back.

5. Which one is true?
   - (A) Pedro could not reach the branch.
   - (B) The bear bit Pedro on the ear.
   - (C) Pedro told Hector a story.
   - (D) The bear climbed up the tree.

Answers

1. (A) (B) (C) (D)
2. (A) (B) (C) (D)
3. (A) (B) (C) (D)
4. (A) (B) (C) (D)
5. (A) (B) (C) (D)

Go on ➤

6. If the bear *really* whispered something to Pedro, this shows that the bear

   Ⓐ was afraid of Pedro.

   Ⓑ was not hungry.

   Ⓒ thought Pedro was dead.

   Ⓓ did not really believe that Pedro was dead.

7. The story says that

   Ⓐ people should think about themselves before they worry about others.

   Ⓑ friends should help each other at all times.

   Ⓒ bears never hurt people.

   Ⓓ you should never walk through the woods alone.

8. The man thought that he and his friend should share the ax. When two people *share* something, they

   Ⓐ find it.

   Ⓑ sell it.

   Ⓒ give it away.

   Ⓓ both use it.

9. Hector ran away because he feared the bear. The word *feared* means

   Ⓐ was afraid of.

   Ⓑ did not like.

   Ⓒ heard about.

   Ⓓ did not know.

10. The huge bear was coming closer and closer. The word *huge* means

   Ⓐ very small.

   Ⓑ very big.

   Ⓒ very young.

   Ⓓ very friendly.

Answers

6.	Ⓐ	Ⓑ	Ⓒ	Ⓓ
7.	Ⓐ	Ⓑ	Ⓒ	Ⓓ
8.	Ⓐ	Ⓑ	Ⓒ	Ⓓ
9.	Ⓐ	Ⓑ	Ⓒ	Ⓓ
10.	Ⓐ	Ⓑ	Ⓒ	Ⓓ

How many questions did you get right? Circle your score below. Then fill in your **Reading Skills** score on the **Test-Taker Score Chart** on the inside of the back cover.

Number Correct	1	2	3	4	5	6	7	8	9	10
My Score	10	20	30	40	50	60	70	80	90	100

Go on ➤

II. Mechanics (capital letters, punctuation, commas, spelling, and grammar)

Fill in the circle next to the right answer.

1. Which sentence needs a capital letter?
   - Ⓐ Pedro and Hector were friends.
   - Ⓑ The men walked through the woods.
   - Ⓒ they saw a big bear.

2. Which sentence has a mistake in punctuation?
   - Ⓐ When did you read the story?
   - Ⓑ Did you like the story.
   - Ⓒ What a great story that was!

3. Which sentence needs a comma?
   - Ⓐ Hector climbed higher and higher.
   - Ⓑ The bear was big, but it was friendly.
   - Ⓒ The man was tall strong, and angry.

4. Which sentence has a word that is spelled wrong? Look at the **underlined** words.
   - Ⓐ The man used the ax for <u>cutting</u> down trees.
   - Ⓑ The bear was <u>runing</u> toward them.
   - Ⓒ The bear <u>stopped</u> and looked at Pedro.

5. Which sentence has a mistake in grammar?
   - Ⓐ They is good friends.
   - Ⓑ They are going to the lake.
   - Ⓒ They saw a bear in the woods.

Answers

1. Ⓐ Ⓑ Ⓒ Ⓓ
2. Ⓐ Ⓑ Ⓒ Ⓓ
3. Ⓐ Ⓑ Ⓒ Ⓓ
4. Ⓐ Ⓑ Ⓒ Ⓓ
5. Ⓐ Ⓑ Ⓒ Ⓓ

How many questions did you get right? Circle your score below. Then fill in your **Mechanics** score on the **Test-Taker Score Chart** on the inside of the back cover.

Number Correct	1	2	3	4	5
Your Score	20	40	60	80	100

Go on ➤

III. Writing

Answer the questions. You may look back at the
story as often as you wish.

1. Pedro said that the bear whispered, "The boy in the
   tree is not your friend. He will not help you when you
   need him." Why did the bear say that to Pedro?

   _____

   _____

   _____

   _____

   _____

2. Do you think the bear *really* whispered something to
   Pedro—or do you think Pedro made that up? Explain
   your answer.

   I think that_____

   _____

   _____

   _____

   _____

   _____

   _____

Go on ➤

3. There are really *two* stories in "Two Good Friends." One story is about two friends and an ax. The other story is about two friends and a bear. How are the stories *alike* (the same)? How are they *different?* List three answers in the chart.

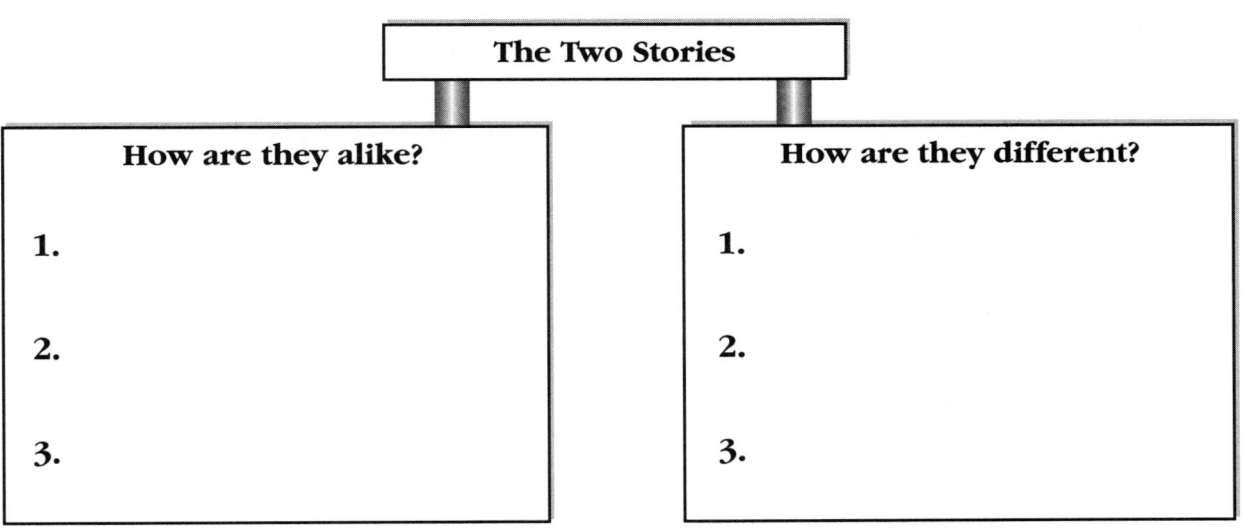

The Two Stories

How are they alike?	How are they different?
1.	1.
2.	2.
3.	3.

4. Write about a friend. Tell what you like about your friend. Tell about some things you do together. Write about a real friend or make one up.

My Friend

_____

_____

_____

_____

_____

_____

Stop

Ride, Sally Ride

It is June 18, 1983. The place is Florida. It is early in the morning. The sun has just come up.

Many people are standing around. Some people have come from far away. Others have come from places that are near. Everyone is excited. Everyone is waiting.

Why have these people come? What are they waiting for?

Far away stands a spaceship. It can fly very high into the sky. It can fly into space.[1]

There is a woman in the spaceship. Sally Ride is her name. She is an astronaut. What is an astronaut? An astronaut is someone who flies into space.

Americans have been in space before. But all of them were men. Today Sally Ride will fly into space. She will be the first American woman in space.

People have heard about Sally Ride. They want to see her fly into space. That is why they came to Florida today.

1. space: the air high above Earth. The moon, stars, and sun are in space.

For additional exercises and another story about flying, see "Two Who Flew" in *Travels* in *Goodman's Five-Star Stories,* Level A.

Many people are wearing bright shirts. The shirts have words on them. The words are very big. The words say, "Ride, Sally Ride."

Sally Ride was born in 1951. She was born in Los Angeles. That is a big city in California.

When she was a girl, she was very good at sports. Sally liked tennis very much. She played for hours every day. People said that she would become a great tennis player.

But Sally liked something even more than tennis. She liked to read about Earth. She liked to read about the stars. Sally often looked up at the stars. She thought they were beautiful. But they were very far away. She did not know that she would fly near them one day.

Later, Sally went to a very good school. It is named Stanford. She learned a lot about space at Stanford.

Then Sally heard about NASA. It teaches people how to become astronauts. Sally sent a letter to NASA. She said she wanted to be an astronaut.

Many other people wanted to be astronauts too. NASA could pick only a few. Sally was one of the people they chose.

There was a NASA school in Texas. Sally moved to Texas. She went to the NASA school. Sally worked very hard. She learned how to fly a plane. She learned how to live in space.

One day NASA said that Sally was ready. She could fly into space! She would be on a spaceship. It would take off from Florida. The day would be June 18, 1983. Sally would be in space. She would live there for six days.

Sally was very happy. She could hardly wait.

June 18, 1983, finally came. Early that morning Sally climbed into the spaceship. Three other astronauts were with her. The other three astronauts were men. Together they got ready to fly. They made sure that everything was working well. They did not want anything to go wrong.

At 7:32 in the morning, the spaceship was all set to go. Its big engines began to roar. The noise was very loud. People who were far away could hear the sound.

Then the spaceship left the ground. It flew higher and higher and higher.

Far away, the people pointed at the sky. They were delighted! They saw what they had come to see. An American woman was flying into space!

Soon the spaceship was in space. It was flying around Earth. It went around Earth in less than two hours!

The astronauts had many things to do. They took pictures. They wrote down what they saw. The time went by very fast.

Six days passed. Then the spaceship came back to Earth. It landed in California. Many people came to see the spaceship land. They saw Sally climb out of the spaceship. They all cheered.

Sally Ride had a great time flying in space. She said, "It was the most fun that I will ever have in my life."

Go on ➤

I. Reading Skills

Fill in the circle next to the right answer.

1. This story is mostly about
   Ⓐ life in space.
   Ⓑ NASA.
   Ⓒ Sally Ride.
   Ⓓ people in Florida.

2. Which sentence is *not* true?
   Ⓐ Sally Ride was born in 1971.
   Ⓑ Sally was good at sports.
   Ⓒ Sally liked to read.
   Ⓓ Sally was the first American woman to fly into space.

3. Sally Ride moved to Texas to
   Ⓐ live with her family.
   Ⓑ go to a NASA school.
   Ⓒ play tennis.
   Ⓓ visit friends.

4. When did the spaceship take off?
   Ⓐ in the morning
   Ⓑ in the afternoon
   Ⓒ after dinner
   Ⓓ at night

5. How long was the spaceship in space?
   Ⓐ less than two hours
   Ⓑ just one day
   Ⓒ six days
   Ⓓ a week

6. "Ride, Sally Ride" shows that astronauts must
   Ⓐ be men.
   Ⓑ come from the United States.
   Ⓒ go to Stanford.
   Ⓓ work together.

Answers

1. Ⓐ Ⓑ Ⓒ Ⓓ
2. Ⓐ Ⓑ Ⓒ Ⓓ
3. Ⓐ Ⓑ Ⓒ Ⓓ
4. Ⓐ Ⓑ Ⓒ Ⓓ
5. Ⓐ Ⓑ Ⓒ Ⓓ
6. Ⓐ Ⓑ Ⓒ Ⓓ

Go on ➤

7. The last line of the story shows that Sally

   Ⓐ did not like her trip in space.

   Ⓑ loved flying in space.

   Ⓒ did not plan to fly into space again.

   Ⓓ was sorry she became an astronaut.

8. Sally was one of the people NASA chose. The word *chose* means

   Ⓐ forgot.

   Ⓑ picked.

   Ⓒ heard.

   Ⓓ stopped.

9. The people were delighted to see the spaceship fly into space. The word *delighted* means

   Ⓐ sorry.

   Ⓑ worried.

   Ⓒ very surprised.

   Ⓓ very happy.

10. They cheered when Sally came out of the spaceship. The word *cheered* means

    Ⓐ yelled with joy.

    Ⓑ went away.

    Ⓒ became angry.

    Ⓓ kept quiet.

Answers

7. Ⓐ Ⓑ Ⓒ Ⓓ
8. Ⓐ Ⓑ Ⓒ Ⓓ
9. Ⓐ Ⓑ Ⓒ Ⓓ
10. Ⓐ Ⓑ Ⓒ Ⓓ

How many questions did you get right? Circle your score below. Then fill in your **Reading Skills** score on the **Test-Taker Score Chart** on the inside of the back cover.

Number Correct	1	2	3	4	5	6	7	8	9	10
My Score		10	20	30	40	50	60	70	80	90	100

Go on ➤

II. Mechanics (capital letters, punctuation, commas, spelling, and grammar)

Fill in the circle next to the right answer.

1. Which sentence needs a capital letter?

   Ⓐ Sally Ride was born in Los Angeles.

   Ⓑ That is a very big city.

   Ⓒ The spaceship landed in california.

2. Which sentence has a mistake in punctuation?

   Ⓐ Did Sally play tennis very well?

   Ⓑ Sally went to a school in Texas.

   Ⓒ She said, "Flying in space is fun"

3. Which sentence needs a comma?

   Ⓐ The day was June 18 1983.

   Ⓑ Sally learned a lot about Earth and space.

   Ⓒ The big spaceship was all set to go.

4. Which sentence has a word that is spelled wrong? Look at the **underlined** words.

   Ⓐ Sally <u>knew</u> a lot about the stars.

   Ⓑ She had many <u>friends</u> in school.

   Ⓒ People who were far away could <u>here</u> the sound.

5. Which sentence has a mistake in grammar?

   Ⓐ The people were very excited.

   Ⓑ They seen the spaceship leave the ground.

   Ⓒ It went into space.

Answers
1. Ⓐ Ⓑ Ⓒ Ⓓ
2. Ⓐ Ⓑ Ⓒ Ⓓ
3. Ⓐ Ⓑ Ⓒ Ⓓ
4. Ⓐ Ⓑ Ⓒ Ⓓ
5. Ⓐ Ⓑ Ⓒ Ⓓ

How many questions did you get right? Circle your score below. Then fill in your **Mechanics** score on the **Test-Taker Score Chart** on the inside of the back cover.

Number Correct	1	2	3	4	5
Your Score	20	40	60	80	100

Go on ➤

III. Writing

Answer the questions. You may look back at the
story as often as you wish.

1. Do you think you would like to be an astronaut?
   Tell why.

   _____

   _____

   _____

   _____

   _____

2. Write a letter to a friend. Tell your friend about
   Sally Ride.

   _____
   (Date)

   Dear _____,
      (Name of your friend)

   _____

   _____

   _____

   _____

   _____

   _____

   Your friend,

   _____

3. Write the beginning of a short story called "My Trip into Space." Use each of the words in the box in your story.

spaceship	**quiet**	**glad**	**small**
stars	**window**	**round**	**laugh**

My Trip into Space

_____

_____

_____

_____

_____

_____

_____

_____

_____

_____

_____

_____

_____

Stop

DIRECTIONS
Read this true story about The Gambia in Africa.
Then answer the questions.

A Trip to The Gambia

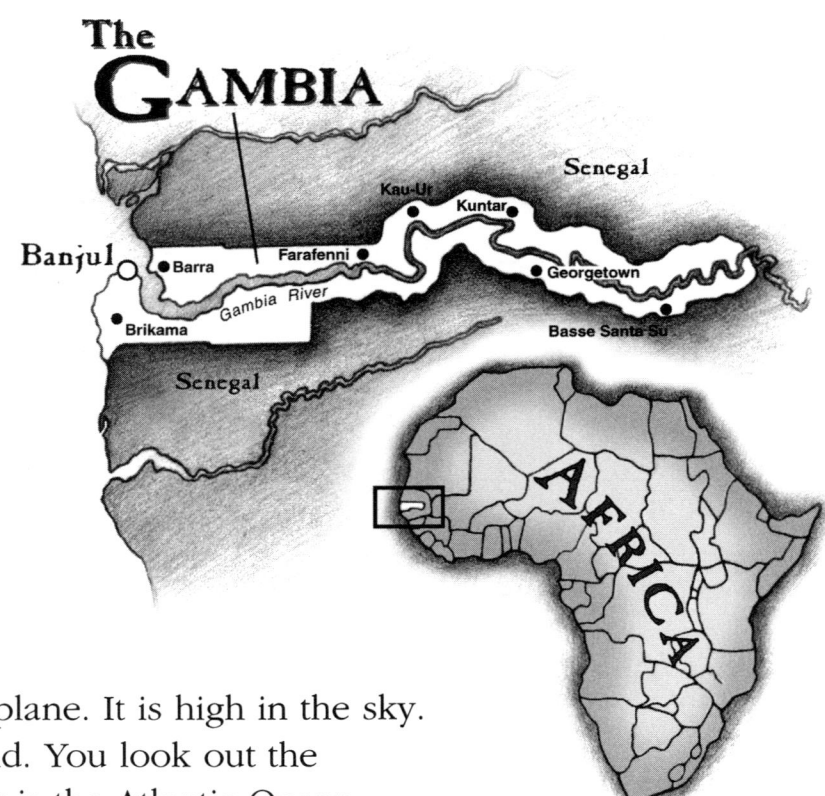

Make believe you are in an airplane. It is high in the sky.
Now it gets closer to the ground. You look out the
window. You see blue water. It is the Atlantic Ocean.

You see people swimming. People are fishing with nets.
There are people sailing. They are in small, wooden boats.

Now you see a beach. The sand on the beach is white.
There are buildings on the beach. The buildings are white
and pink. They shine in the sun.

Your plane is coming into Africa. It will land in a
country called The Gambia. Look at a map of Africa. You
will see The Gambia on the west side of Africa.

The Gambia is a small country. It is only about 30 miles
wide. Most of the time it is very hot in The Gambia. It also
rains a lot there. The Gambia gets about 40 inches of rain
a year. It rains mostly in the summer. That is from June to
October.

For additional exercises and some stories from West Africa, see "Morning
Sunshine" in *Travels* and "Yes I Can" in *More Travels* in *Goodman's Five-Star
Stories,* Level A.

Now your plane is landing in Banjul. Banjul is the largest city in The Gambia. About 45,000 people live there. In Banjul you will see many stores and big buildings.

Banjul is an exciting city to visit. Everywhere people are on the move. But they will be happy to stop and talk to you. They will tell you how to find your way around the city.

There is a big market in Banjul. It is called the Albert Market. You can buy all kinds of clothes and food there.

Many artists sell their paintings at the Albert Market. You can also buy different kinds of masks. The masks are made out of shiny black wood.

After a while you will get hungry. You will want to eat. There is a lot of good food in Banjul. The food is served in large wooden bowls. Many people like black beans and rice. You may want to try that.

You may want to eat fish in Banjul. The city is on the Atlantic Ocean. So you know that the fish is fresh. Sometimes people cook fish over an open fire. You might like the fish cooked that way.

There is a big river in The Gambia. It is called the Gambia River. It is about 700 miles long. The river runs through the center of the country.

At Banjul you can take a boat down the Gambia River. You will see many interesting things along the way.

You will see women working by the river. They are washing clothes in the water. You will see people working in the fields. They are growing vegetables. People are also picking fruit from the trees.

Soon you will come to a town. It is called Kau-Ur. You will see a very unusual thing here. You will see many big stones. The stones are in groups. Each group of stones makes a big circle.

The stones are about five feet high. They are dark red. They are round and have flat tops. The stones are very heavy. The stones are very old. The stone circles are also very old. They are probably more than 1,000 years old.

No one really knows who made the stone circles. People who made them lived long ago We do not know much about those people. We do not know how they lived. We do not know why they made the stone circles.

People have found things in the ground near the stone circles. People have found old bones and old dishes in the ground. The dishes were made long, long ago.

Now it is time to leave. Someday you might come back to The Gambia. But the next time, the trip will not be in your mind. The next time, the trip will be for real!

Go on ➤

I. Reading Skills

Fill in the circle next to the right answer.

1. This story is mostly about
   Ⓐ Africa.
   Ⓑ the Albert Market.
   Ⓒ a boat ride.
   Ⓓ The Gambia.

2. Which one is true?
   Ⓐ It does not rain a lot in The Gambia.
   Ⓑ The Gambia is a very big country.
   Ⓒ Most of the time it is very hot in The Gambia.
   Ⓓ People in The Gambia are not friendly.

3. How long is The Gambia River?
   Ⓐ about 30 miles long
   Ⓑ about 70 miles long
   Ⓒ about 700 miles long
   Ⓓ about 1,000 miles long

4. Most people go to Kau-Ur to
   Ⓐ eat black beans and rice.
   Ⓑ see the stone circles.
   Ⓒ buy clothes at the Albert Market.
   Ⓓ cook fish over an open fire.

5. The stones in the stone circles are
   Ⓐ white and pink.
   Ⓑ about two feet high.
   Ⓒ about five feet high.
   Ⓓ not very heavy.

6. What have people found near the stone circles?
   Ⓐ old dishes
   Ⓑ paintings
   Ⓒ food
   Ⓓ masks made out of wood

Answers				
1.	Ⓐ	Ⓑ	Ⓒ	Ⓓ
2.	Ⓐ	Ⓑ	Ⓒ	Ⓓ
3.	Ⓐ	Ⓑ	Ⓒ	Ⓓ
4.	Ⓐ	Ⓑ	Ⓒ	Ⓓ
5.	Ⓐ	Ⓑ	Ⓒ	Ⓓ
6.	Ⓐ	Ⓑ	Ⓒ	Ⓓ

Go on ➤

7. Who made the stone circles?

  Ⓐ People who lived in Banjul made them.

  Ⓑ People who lived a few years ago made them.

  Ⓒ Visitors from another country made them.

  Ⓓ No one really knows.

8. The sand on the beach is white. A *beach* is

  Ⓐ a road.

  Ⓑ a small woods.

  Ⓒ the land next to an ocean.

  Ⓓ a lake.

9. You can buy many things at the market. As used here, the word *market* means

  Ⓐ a large store.

  Ⓑ a truck.

  Ⓒ a beautiful house.

  Ⓓ a garden.

10. The stone circles are very unusual. The word *unusual* means

  Ⓐ little.

  Ⓑ new.

  Ⓒ bright.

  Ⓓ different.

Answers

7. Ⓐ Ⓑ Ⓒ Ⓓ

8. Ⓐ Ⓑ Ⓒ Ⓓ

9. Ⓐ Ⓑ Ⓒ Ⓓ

10. Ⓐ Ⓑ Ⓒ Ⓓ

How many questions did you get right? Circle your score below. Then fill in your **Reading Skills** score on the **Test-Taker Score Chart** on the inside of the back cover.

Number Correct	1	2	3	4	5	6	7	8	9	10
My Score	10	20	30	40	50	60	70	80	90	100

Go on ➤

II. Mechanics (capital letters, punctuation, commas, spelling, and grammar)

Fill in the circle next to the right answer.

1. Which sentence needs a capital letter?

   Ⓐ You can buy clothes and food at the market.

   Ⓑ It rains a lot from June to October.

   Ⓒ The city is near the atlantic Ocean.

2. Which sentence has a mistake in punctuation?

   Ⓐ Didn't you find the story interesting?

   Ⓑ I can't wait to go there.

   Ⓒ We dont know who made the stone circles.

3. Which sentence needs a comma or does not use the comma correctly?

   Ⓐ The people are busy, but they will help you.

   Ⓑ The stones are round but they have flat tops.

   Ⓒ There were people swimming, fishing, and sailing.

4. Which sentence has a word that is spelled wrong? Look at the **underlined** words.

   Ⓐ The plane is <u>comeing</u> into Banjul.

   Ⓑ We enjoyed <u>taking</u> pictures of the city.

   Ⓒ I am <u>hoping</u> to visit The Gambia again.

5. Which sentence has a mistake in grammar?

   Ⓐ Farmers were working in the fields.

   Ⓑ Women was washing clothes in the river.

   Ⓒ The stone circles are very old.

Answers
1. Ⓐ Ⓑ Ⓒ Ⓓ
2. Ⓐ Ⓑ Ⓒ Ⓓ
3. Ⓐ Ⓑ Ⓒ Ⓓ
4. Ⓐ Ⓑ Ⓒ Ⓓ
5. Ⓐ Ⓑ Ⓒ Ⓓ

How many questions did you get right? Circle your score below. Then fill in your **Mechanics** score on the **Test-Taker Score Chart** on the inside of the back cover.

Number Correct	1	2	3	4	5
Your Score	20	40	60	80	100

Go on ➤

III. Writing

Answer the questions. You may look back at the
story as often as you wish.

1. In the circles below, write five facts (things that are
   true) about The Gambia.

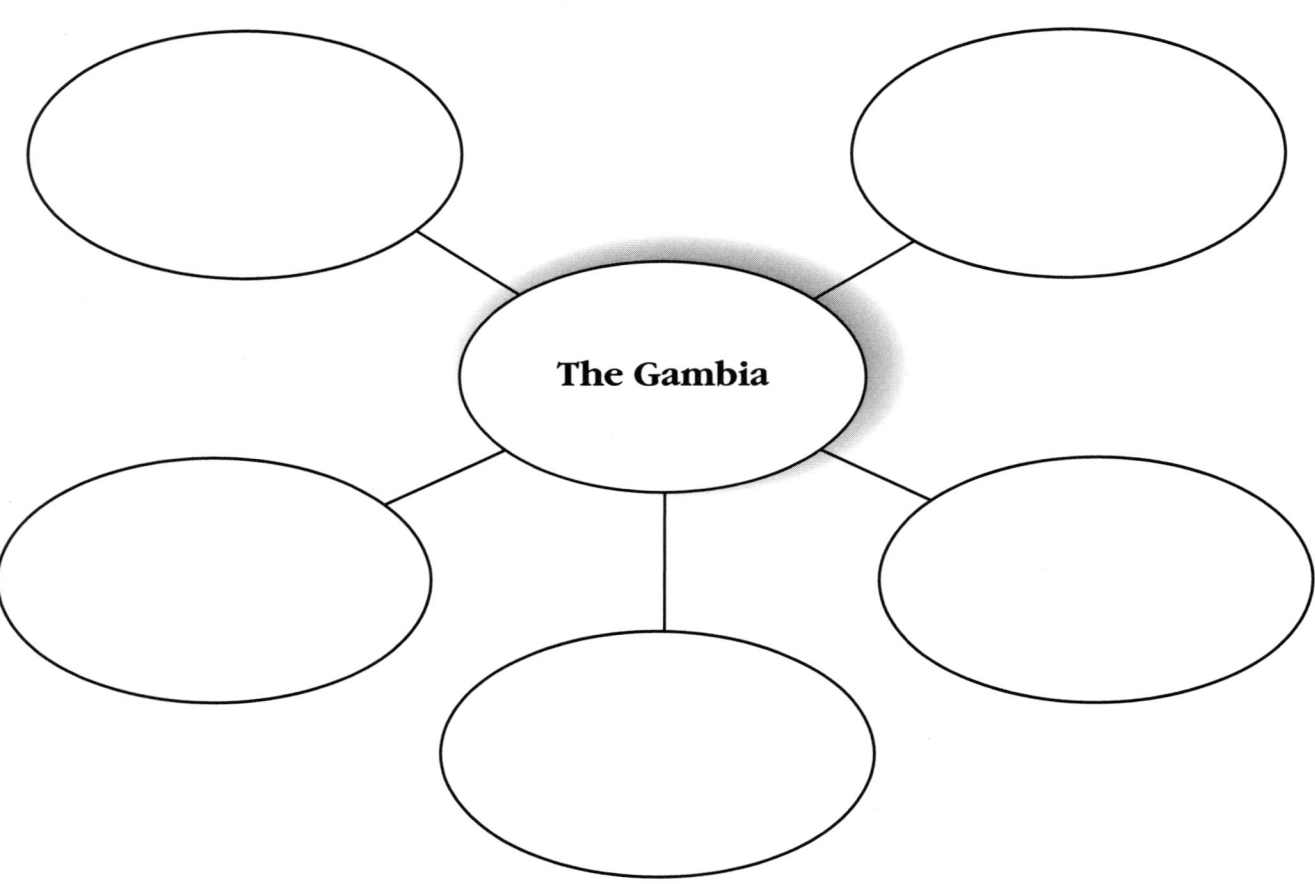

The Gambia

Go on ➤

2. On the lines below, tell about The Gambia. Use some of the facts that you wrote in the circles.

_____

_____

_____

_____

_____

3. Write about a place that you would like to visit. Tell why you would like to go there. What would you like to see and do?

A Place I Would Like to Visit

_____

_____

_____

_____

_____

_____

_____

_____

_____

_____

Go on ➤

IV. Study Skills

Reading a Chart. The Gambia River is not one of the longest rivers in the world. But it is not a small river. It is longer than most rivers. Read the chart below. Then answer the questions.

Some of the World's Longest Rivers			
Name of the river	How long the river is	Where the river begins	What the river goes into
Nile	4,160 miles	Africa	Mediterranean Sea
Amazon	4,000 miles	Peru	Atlantic Ocean
Congo	2,720 miles	Zaire	Atlantic Ocean
Missouri	2,466 miles	Montana	Mississippi River
Mississippi	2,340 miles	Minnesota	Gulf of Mexico

1. How long is the Nile River?

_____

2. How long is the Amazon River?

_____

3. How many miles long is the Mississippi River?

_____

4. Where does the Amazon River begin?

_____

Go on ➤

5. Where does the Missouri River begin?

_____

6. What does the Mississippi River go into?

_____

7. What river goes into the Mediterranean Sea?

_____

8. What two rivers go into the Atlantic Ocean?

_____

9. Which river begins in Zaire?

_____

10. Name the longest river in the world.

_____

The Room

Mrs. Ling lived in China. But she traveled all the time. She had been to many countries. She often went to the United States.

One day Mrs. Ling was at work. She was at her desk. Her boss came into the office. She said, "We need to send you to San Francisco for three days. Then you must go to New York City for four days. Can you leave on Wednesday?"

"Of course," said Mrs. Ling.

Mrs. Ling was happy to go. She loved both cities. She had visited them many times before.

Mrs. Ling talked to her boss. She found out what she had to do. She prepared everything she needed. Then she made a telephone call. She called a hotel[1] in San Francisco. She told them that she was coming.

On Tuesday evening Mrs. Ling packed her bags. She

---

1. hotel: a large building where people pay for a room where they can sleep when they are away from home.

For additional exercises and another story about a visitor, see "The Driver" in *More Travels* in *Goodman's Five-Star Stories,* Level A.

was very excited. She could hardly wait to go.

On Wednesday Mrs. Ling left for San Francisco. She did a lot of work when she was there. She did not see much of the city. The time went by much too quickly.

Then Mrs. Ling left for New York City. The plane landed at Kennedy Airport. She got her bags. Then she called for a cab.

Mrs. Ling got into the cab. "Where do you want to go?" the driver asked.

Mrs. Ling told the driver the name of a hotel. Mrs. Ling liked that hotel. She always stayed there when she was in

New York City.

Mrs. Ling rode in the cab. She said softly to herself, "New York is fun. There is so much to do. There are great places to go. Maybe I can see a show. Maybe I will do some shopping."

Soon the cab stopped at the hotel. Mrs. Ling went inside. She walked to the front desk. She had seen the man at the front desk before. The man at the desk remembered her.

"Hello, Mrs. Ling," he said.

"Hello, Aziz," said Mrs. Ling. "I would like a room. I will be staying here for four days."

There was a computer on the desk. Aziz looked at the computer. He looked very carefully. But he did not see Mrs. Ling's name anywhere.

Aziz was unhappy. He said, "Mrs. Ling, you should have let us know that you were coming. We would have saved a room for you. Now we are full. We have no rooms at all."

"No rooms at all?" said Mrs. Ling.

"No rooms at all. New York City is very, very busy now. All the hotels are filled."

Mrs. Ling said, "But you must have *one* room, Aziz."

Aziz said, "I am sorry, Mrs. Ling. We do not have even one room."

Mrs. Ling thought for a moment. She knew that every hotel saves a room for an important person who might come by.

She said, "Aziz. Suppose that the President came here right now. Surely you would have a room for him."

"The President?" said Aziz. "Well, of course. The President! We have a room for him."

"Well, then," said Mrs. Ling. "I was listening to the radio in the cab. The President will be in Washington tonight. You can give me his room."

A big smile crossed Aziz's face. "All right. You win, Mrs. Ling," he said. He reached for a key and gave it to her.

Mrs. Ling had a *very* good room that night.

Go on ➤

I. Reading Skills

Fill in the circle next to the right answer.

1. This story is mostly about
   Ⓐ why Mrs. Ling went to the United States.
   Ⓑ things to do in New York City.
   Ⓒ how Mrs. Ling got a room in a hotel.
   Ⓓ what Mrs. Ling did at work.

2. Which words belong in Box 1?
   Ⓐ did not like to take trips
   Ⓑ met the President
   Ⓒ saw some shows in San Francisco
   Ⓓ loved New York City

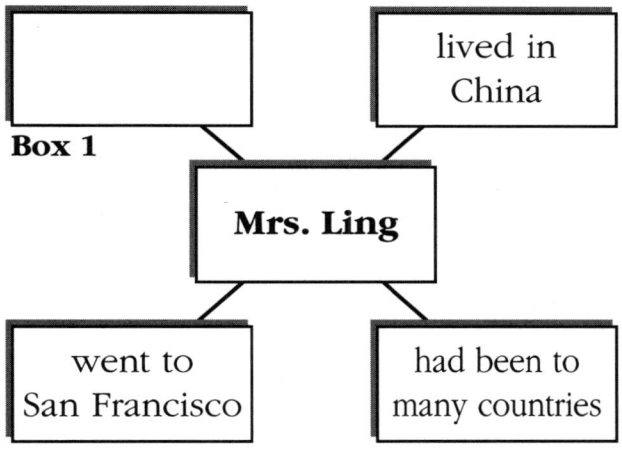

Box 1

lived in China

Mrs. Ling

went to San Francisco

had been to many countries

3. Mrs. Ling always stayed at the same hotel because she
   Ⓐ was afraid to go to a different hotel.
   Ⓑ did not know the name of any other hotel.

Ⓒ did not know where to find another hotel.
Ⓓ liked that hotel very much.

4. Which one is true?
   Ⓐ Aziz did not remember Mrs. Ling.
   Ⓑ Mrs. Ling remembered Aziz.
   Ⓒ Aziz looked for and found Mrs. Ling's name.
   Ⓓ Mrs. Ling had never been to New York City before.

5. Mrs. Ling should have
   Ⓐ called the hotel in New York before she left China.
   Ⓑ left San Francisco a day or two earlier.
   Ⓒ told Aziz that she would not leave until he gave her a room.
   Ⓓ yelled at Aziz until he gave her a room.

Answers

1. Ⓐ Ⓑ Ⓒ Ⓓ
2. Ⓐ Ⓑ Ⓒ Ⓓ
3. Ⓐ Ⓑ Ⓒ Ⓓ
4. Ⓐ Ⓑ Ⓒ Ⓓ
5. Ⓐ Ⓑ Ⓒ Ⓓ

Go on ➤

6. Aziz would have given a room to the President because

Ⓐ Aziz and the President were very good friends.

Ⓑ the President always stayed at that hotel.

Ⓒ the President is very important.

Ⓓ the President was willing to pay a lot of money for the room.

7. The story shows that Mrs. Ling

Ⓐ could think very fast.

Ⓑ did not work hard.

Ⓒ was not able to stay in New York City.

Ⓓ was sorry she came to the United States.

8. Mrs. Ling traveled to many countries. The word *traveled* means

Ⓐ knew about.

Ⓑ went from place to place.

Ⓒ had many friends.

Ⓓ sent letters to.

9. She prepared everything she needed for the trip. The word *prepared* means

Ⓐ got ready.

Ⓑ liked.

Ⓒ left early.

Ⓓ lost.

10. Mrs. Ling got her bags and called for a cab. What is a *cab?*

Ⓐ an airplane

Ⓑ a train

Ⓒ a boat

Ⓓ a car

Answers

6.	Ⓐ	Ⓑ	Ⓒ	Ⓓ
7.	Ⓐ	Ⓑ	Ⓒ	Ⓓ
8.	Ⓐ	Ⓑ	Ⓒ	Ⓓ
9.	Ⓐ	Ⓑ	Ⓒ	Ⓓ
10.	Ⓐ	Ⓑ	Ⓒ	Ⓓ

How many questions did you get right? Circle your score below. Then fill in your **Reading Skills** score on the **Test-Taker Score Chart** on the inside of the back cover.

Number Correct	1	2	3	4	5	6	7	8	9	10
My Score	10	20	30	40	50	60	70	80	90	100

Go on ➤

II. Mechanics (capital letters, punctuation, commas, spelling, and grammar)

Fill in the circle next to the right answer.

1. Which sentence needs a capital letter?
   - Ⓐ Mrs. Ling had been to many countries.
   - Ⓑ Mrs. Ling packed her bags on tuesday.
   - Ⓒ On Wednesday she went to the airport.

2. Which sentence has a mistake in punctuation?
   - Ⓐ Aziz did not see Mrs. Lings name.
   - Ⓑ The driver's car was new.
   - Ⓒ The plane's engines made a loud noise.

3. Which sentence needs a comma?
   - Ⓐ Mrs. Ling went to San Francisco California.
   - Ⓑ She sat in the plane and read.
   - Ⓒ The President was in Washington, D.C.

4. Which sentence has a word that is spelled wrong? Look at the **underlined** words.
   - Ⓐ Mrs. Ling loves to visit <u>cities</u>.
   - Ⓑ She <u>allways</u> stays at the same hotel.
   - Ⓒ A big smile <u>crossed</u> Aziz's face.

5. Which one has a mistake in grammar?
   - Ⓐ Mrs. Ling rode to the airport.
   - Ⓑ She stayed in San Francisco. And New York City.
   - Ⓒ Then she flew back to China.

Answers

1. Ⓐ Ⓑ Ⓒ Ⓓ
2. Ⓐ Ⓑ Ⓒ Ⓓ
3. Ⓐ Ⓑ Ⓒ Ⓓ
4. Ⓐ Ⓑ Ⓒ Ⓓ
5. Ⓐ Ⓑ Ⓒ Ⓓ

How many questions did you get right? Circle your score below. Then fill in your **Mechanics** score on the **Test-Taker Score Chart** on the inside of the back cover.

Number Correct	1	2	3	4	5
Your Score	20	40	60	80	100

Go on ➤

III. Writing

Answer the questions. You may look back at the
story as often as you wish.

1. Why was Mrs. Ling happy to go to the United States?

_____

_____

_____

_____

2. Why didn't Mrs. Ling see much of San Francisco?

_____

_____

_____

_____

3. Aziz was unhappy after he looked at the computer on
   the desk. Explain why Aziz was unhappy.

_____

_____

_____

_____

Go on ➤

4. Mrs. Ling had "a *very* good room" that night.
   Explain why.

   _____

   _____

   _____

5. Tell about the city, town, or village where you live.
   What are some interesting places to see? What are
   some things to do? If you wish, tell about some
   interesting people you know.

   The Place I Live

   _____

   _____

   _____

   _____

   _____

   _____

   _____

   _____

   _____

Stop

The Life of the Rain Forest

At first everything seems quiet. It is very dark. Tall trees are all around you. Their leaves keep out most of the sun's light.

The air is very hot. It is not raining now. But the air seems filled with rain.

Then you begin to hear sounds. Birds sing above you. A frog calls out. A monkey swings from a tree.

You see a snake. It moves along the ground. Ants march across a plant. Large flowers are growing. The flowers are beautiful. They have very bright colors.

You are in a rain forest. There is life all around you. Everything seems fine. But it is really not fine. The rain forest is in danger. It is in very great danger!

Here are some things you should know.

Rain forests grow where there is plenty of rain. How much rain falls in a rain forest? In some years there are

For additional exercises and a story with a similar setting, see "The Queen's Garden" in *Travels* in *Goodman's Five-Star Stories,* Level A.

about 100 inches of rain. In other years 400 inches of rain will fall.

There are rain forests in South America, Asia, and Africa. These forests are very big. Suppose that you could put them all together. They would be almost as big as the United States.

The largest rain forest is in the Amazon. Most of the Amazon is in Brazil. Brazil is a country in South America.

Many of the world's plants and animals live in rain forests. Think of a very small part of an Amazon rain forest. It might be the size of two football fields. It would have more than 200 different kinds of trees. Most forests in the United States have about 10 kinds of trees.

Rain forests have more than animals and plants. Many people live in rain forests too. People have made their homes in rain forests for many, many years.

These people *need* the rain forests to live. The people eat the plants. They hunt the animals. They use the trees and animals to make their clothes. They use the trees and plants to build their homes.

Many good things also come from rain forests. Plants in rain forests are used to make medicines. The medicines help sick people get better. Many kinds of fruits and nuts are found only in rain forests. The fruits and nuts are sold all over the world.

People need the rain forests. But the forests are getting smaller and smaller. Many are dying! Someday we may not even have rain forests!

Why? Are the forests dying because they do not get enough sun? Do they need more rain?

No. The forests are dying because of people. Some people want the wood from the rain forests very much. These people chop down many trees in the forest. Then they sell the wood.

Other people who live near rain forests have cattle. They want land where their cattle can live. Cattle cannot live in land filled with trees. Cattle need land that has grass.

Some farmers burn down large parts of the forest. When the trees are gone, cattle can live on the land.

People burn trees in rain forests every day. Every minute, trees are being burned in rain forests somewhere.

It is not good to burn too many trees. When a tree burns, a gas goes into the air. This gas makes the air warmer. If there is too much gas in the air, the air will get hotter.

People who study the air are worried. They think that the world's air is becoming too warm. They believe this will be bad for all living things.

Without the rain forests, many plants and animals will die. People who live in the rain forests will lose their homes. And if people keep burning trees, the air may get too hot. We might not be able to live.

Yes, rain forests are very important. That is why so many people are trying to save them.

I. Reading Skills

Fill in the circle next to the right answer.

1. This story says that rain forests are
   - Ⓐ dying.
   - Ⓑ not important.
   - Ⓒ very small.
   - Ⓓ too big.

2. It is dark in a rain forest because
   - Ⓐ it rains there every day.
   - Ⓑ trees and leaves keep out the light.
   - Ⓒ it is filled with beautiful flowers.
   - Ⓓ there are animals everywhere.

3. Which one is true?
   - Ⓐ People cannot live in rain forests.
   - Ⓑ Rain forests do not get enough rain.
   - Ⓒ There are no snakes in rain forests.
   - Ⓓ Many animals and plants live in rain forests.

4. The biggest rain forest is in
   - Ⓐ Asia.
   - Ⓑ Africa.
   - Ⓒ the Amazon.
   - Ⓓ the United States.

5. Why are rain forests getting smaller?
   - Ⓐ They need more sun and rain.
   - Ⓑ People are cutting and burning trees.
   - Ⓒ More and more people are moving there.
   - Ⓓ Animals keep eating the plants and the trees.

6. What may happen if too many trees are burned?
   - Ⓐ The air may get too cold.
   - Ⓑ The air may get too warm.
   - Ⓒ Cattle will have no place to live.
   - Ⓓ It may rain all the time.

Answers

1. Ⓐ Ⓑ Ⓒ Ⓓ
2. Ⓐ Ⓑ Ⓒ Ⓓ
3. Ⓐ Ⓑ Ⓒ Ⓓ
4. Ⓐ Ⓑ Ⓒ Ⓓ
5. Ⓐ Ⓑ Ⓒ Ⓓ
6. Ⓐ Ⓑ Ⓒ Ⓓ

Go on ➤

7. The last two lines of the story say that rain forests are

    Ⓐ very beautiful.

    Ⓑ home to many people.

    Ⓒ good and should be saved.

    Ⓓ safe right now.

8. Rain forests grow where there is plenty of rain. The word *plenty* means

    Ⓐ a lot of.

    Ⓑ not much.

    Ⓒ some.

    Ⓓ none at all.

9. They chop down the trees and sell the wood. The word *chop* means

    Ⓐ burn.

    Ⓑ pull.

    Ⓒ cut.

    Ⓓ buy.

10. Some people are worried because they think that the air may get too warm. When you are *worried*, you

    Ⓐ are glad.

    Ⓑ are sad.

    Ⓒ do not care.

    Ⓓ feel a little afraid.

Answers

7. Ⓐ Ⓑ Ⓒ Ⓓ

8. Ⓐ Ⓑ Ⓒ Ⓓ

9. Ⓐ Ⓑ Ⓒ Ⓓ

10. Ⓐ Ⓑ Ⓒ Ⓓ

How many questions did you get right? Circle your score below. Then fill in your **Reading Skills** score on the **Test-Taker Score Chart** on the inside of the back cover.

Number Correct	1	2	3	4	5	6	7	8	9	10
My Score	10	20	30	40	50	60	70	80	90	100

Go on ➤

II. Mechanics (capital letters, punctuation, commas, spelling, and grammar)

Fill in the circle next to the right answer.

1. Which sentence needs a capital letter?
   - Ⓐ Many plants and animals live in rain forests.
   - Ⓑ There are rain forests in South America and asia.
   - Ⓒ There are also rain forests in Africa.

2. Which sentence is not punctuated correctly?
   - Ⓐ Look out for that falling tree!
   - Ⓑ Dr. R. W. Rivera writes about rain forests.
   - Ⓒ Mr and Mrs Chu went to a rain forest in Brazil.

3. Which sentence needs a comma or does not use the comma correctly?
   - Ⓐ Birds, snakes, and frogs live in rain forests.
   - Ⓑ Trees and flowers are also found there.
   - Ⓒ There are no rain forests in London England.

4. Which sentence has a word that is spelled wrong? Look at the **underlined** words.
   - Ⓐ People should not burn <u>too</u> many trees.
   - Ⓑ Gas from the burning trees may make the air <u>to</u> warm.
   - Ⓒ Is Earth <u>getting</u> hotter and hotter?

5. Which sentence has a mistake in grammar?
   - Ⓐ Many large flowers grows in the rain forests.
   - Ⓑ The flowers have very bright colors.
   - Ⓒ They look like paintings.

Answers

1. Ⓐ Ⓑ Ⓒ Ⓓ
2. Ⓐ Ⓑ Ⓒ Ⓓ
3. Ⓐ Ⓑ Ⓒ Ⓓ
4. Ⓐ Ⓑ Ⓒ Ⓓ
5. Ⓐ Ⓑ Ⓒ Ⓓ

How many questions did you get right? Circle your score below. Then fill in your **Mechanics** score on the **Test-Taker Score Chart** on the inside of the back cover.

Number Correct	1	2	3	4	5
Your Score	20	40	60	80	100

Go on ➤

III. Writing

Answer the questions. You may look back at the
story as often as you wish.

1. This story tells you facts (things that are true) about
   rain forests. In the box below, list five facts about rain
   forests.

Five Things That Are True About Rain Forests

1.

2.

3.

4.

5.

2. Do you think that people should try to save rain forests? Tell why.

_____

_____

_____

_____

_____

_____

_____

Go on ➤

3. Make believe that you are walking in a rain forest. Tell where the rain forest is. Then tell about all the things that you see, hear, smell, taste, and feel.

My Walk in a Rain Forest

_____

_____

_____

_____

_____

_____

_____

_____

_____

_____

_____

_____

_____

_____

Stop

DIRECTIONS
A fable is a story that teaches a lesson. Read the fable.
Then answer the questions.

Belling the Cat

an Aesop's fable

Who was Aesop? We do not know for sure. We do not even know if Aesop ever really lived.

Many people think that he did live. They believe that he lived many years ago. They think he lived in Greece.

They believe that Aesop was a very wise man. They say he made up fables. A fable is a very short story that teaches a lesson. Aesop told the fables to people. Later, people wrote down Aesop's stories.

Aesop's fables are very, very old. They may be more than 2,000 years old. But people still enjoy these stories today.

Aesop's fables always end with a lesson. The stories teach something. Maybe that is why people like them so much.

"Belling the Cat" is one of Aesop's most famous stories. Look for the lesson at the end of the fable.

For additional exercises and other stories involving problems and solutions, see "The King and the Shoemaker" in *Travels* and "Answer Me This" in *More Travels* in *Goodman's Five-Star Stories,* Level A.

Years ago, many mice lived in a big house. The mice lived a good life. It was warm in the house. It was dry in the house. There was always a lot of food around.

An old man and his wife lived in the house. They did not mind the mice. They did not care about the mice.

The mice did what they wanted to do. They ran up and down the stairs. They went into all the rooms. They were not afraid of anything. Nobody ever bothered them.

Things went on this way for many years. The mice were very happy. They loved living in the house.

Then one day something happened. The man and his wife got a pet. The pet was a cat.

Well! Life suddenly changed for the mice. It was not a change for the better. The cat was very big and very clever. It moved quietly about. It did not make a sound. It moved very quickly. Then suddenly it jumped. It caught and killed a mouse.

Day after day, the cat killed mice. The mice were afraid all the time.

At last a few mice said, "It is time to do something. Let us hold a meeting. All the mice must come. We will talk about the cat. Maybe we can think of a way to save ourselves."

The mice held a big meeting. All the mice were there. They talked about what to do. Some of the mice had ideas. But none of the ideas seemed very good.

Then a young mouse spoke up. He said, "The problem is this. The cat is very quiet. We cannot tell where he is or when he is coming. But I have a plan. It is a very good plan. It will save us from the cat."

All the mice sat up. They listened with great interest.

"It is very simple," said the young mouse. "We must tie a bell around the cat's neck. When we hear the bell ring, we will know that the cat is near. Then we can run away. The cat will not catch us."

"That is a great idea!" shouted the mice. "The bell will tell us that the cat is near."

The mice clapped their paws. They cried out, "We are saved! We are saved!"

Then an old mouse stood up. "Excuse me, please," he said. "That sounds like a very fine plan. But before we clap and cheer, please tell me this. Which mouse will tie the bell on the cat?"

The mice looked at each other. They were silent. No one said a word. You could not hear a mouse squeak.

Then the old mouse said, "There is a lesson here. The lesson is this: *Some things are easier said than done.*"

Go on >

I. Reading Skills

Fill in the circle next to the right answer.

1. This story is mostly about
   Ⓐ the life of Aesop.
   Ⓑ an old man and his wife.
   Ⓒ a young mouse.
   Ⓓ a plan for saving mice from a cat.

2. Many people believe that Aesop
   Ⓐ lived a few years ago.
   Ⓑ came from Greece.
   Ⓒ was not smart.
   Ⓓ made up long stories.

3. Why did the mice have a meeting?
   Ⓐ to see what they could do about the cat
   Ⓑ to find a place to hide
   Ⓒ to look for a new place to live
   Ⓓ to talk about where to find food

4. Which sentence is *not* true?
   Ⓐ The cat was big.
   Ⓑ The cat was clever.
   Ⓒ The cat did not make a sound.
   Ⓓ The cat always moved slowly.

5. We know that the cat killed many mice because
   Ⓐ the mice were afraid of the cat.
   Ⓑ there were many mice in the house.
   Ⓒ the cat killed mice day after day.
   Ⓓ the cat said, "I have killed many mice."

6. The young mouse's plan could *not* work because
   Ⓐ the mice did not have a bell.
   Ⓑ the cat was already wearing a bell.
   Ⓒ no mouse would tie the bell on the cat.
   Ⓓ some mice would not be able to hear the bell ring.

Answers

1. Ⓐ Ⓑ Ⓒ Ⓓ
2. Ⓐ Ⓑ Ⓒ Ⓓ
3. Ⓐ Ⓑ Ⓒ Ⓓ
4. Ⓐ Ⓑ Ⓒ Ⓓ
5. Ⓐ Ⓑ Ⓒ Ⓓ
6. Ⓐ Ⓑ Ⓒ Ⓓ

Go on ➤

7. "Belling the Cat" teaches us that
   Ⓐ most plans are not good.
   Ⓑ some ideas sound good, but they will not work.
   Ⓒ you should be happy with what you have.
   Ⓓ it is easy to find good ideas.

8. Aesop's stories end with a lesson. What does a *lesson* do?
   Ⓐ It makes you feel sad.
   Ⓑ It always makes you laugh.
   Ⓒ It makes you feel angry.
   Ⓓ It teaches you something.

9. "Belling the Cat" is a very famous story. When something is *famous*,
   Ⓐ it is new.
   Ⓑ it is funny.
   Ⓒ many people know about it.
   Ⓓ few people know about it.

10. The mice did not say a word. All of them were silent. The word *silent* means
   Ⓐ quiet.
   Ⓑ happy.
   Ⓒ tired.
   Ⓓ afraid.

Answers

7.	Ⓐ	Ⓑ	Ⓒ	Ⓓ
8.	Ⓐ	Ⓑ	Ⓒ	Ⓓ
9.	Ⓐ	Ⓑ	Ⓒ	Ⓓ
10.	Ⓐ	Ⓑ	Ⓒ	Ⓓ

How many questions did you get right? Circle your score below. Then fill in your **Reading Skills** score on the **Test-Taker Score Chart** on the inside of the back cover.

Number Correct	1	2	3	4	5	6	7	8	9	10
My Score	10	20	30	40	50	60	70	80	90	100

Go on ➤

II. Mechanics (capital letters, punctuation, commas, spelling, and grammar)

Fill in the circle next to the right answer.

1. Which sentence is not capitalized correctly?
   - Ⓐ The name of this story is "belling the cat."
   - Ⓑ It is a story that was told by Aesop.
   - Ⓒ His stories are read in schools all over the world.

2. Which sentence is not punctuated correctly?
   - Ⓐ The young mouse said, "I have a good plan."
   - Ⓑ The old mouse asked, Which mouse will tie the bell on the cat?
   - Ⓒ Why didn't the young mouse's plan work?

3. Which sentence needs a comma or does not use the comma correctly?
   - Ⓐ The cat was big, but it moved very quickly.
   - Ⓑ Have you read any other stories by Aesop Marie?
   - Ⓒ Yes, I have read other stories by Aesop.

4. Which sentence has a word that is spelled wrong? Look at the **underlined** words.
   - Ⓐ They brought a cat into <u>their</u> house.
   - Ⓑ The mice did not <u>know</u> what to do.
   - Ⓒ The mice clapped <u>there</u> paws.

5. Which sentence has a mistake in grammar?
   - Ⓐ Many people have heard Aesop's stories.
   - Ⓑ The mice were very happy.
   - Ⓒ They done what they wanted to do.

Answers

1.	Ⓐ	Ⓑ	Ⓒ	Ⓓ
2.	Ⓐ	Ⓑ	Ⓒ	Ⓓ
3.	Ⓐ	Ⓑ	Ⓒ	Ⓓ
4.	Ⓐ	Ⓑ	Ⓒ	Ⓓ
5.	Ⓐ	Ⓑ	Ⓒ	Ⓓ

How many questions did you get right? Circle your score below. Then fill in your **Mechanics** score on the **Test-Taker Score Chart** on the inside of the back cover.

Number Correct	1	2	3	4	5
Your Score	20	40	60	80	100

Go on ➤

III. Writing

Answer the questions. You may look back at the
story as often as you wish.

1. Explain the young mouse's plan for saving the mice.

_____

_____

_____

_____

_____

2. In "Belling the Cat" the old man and his wife got a cat
   as a pet. That was not good for the mice. Perhaps you
   have a pet or know people who have pets. What are
   some good things about having a pet? What are some
   things that are *not* very good? In the chart below, list as
   many answers as you can.

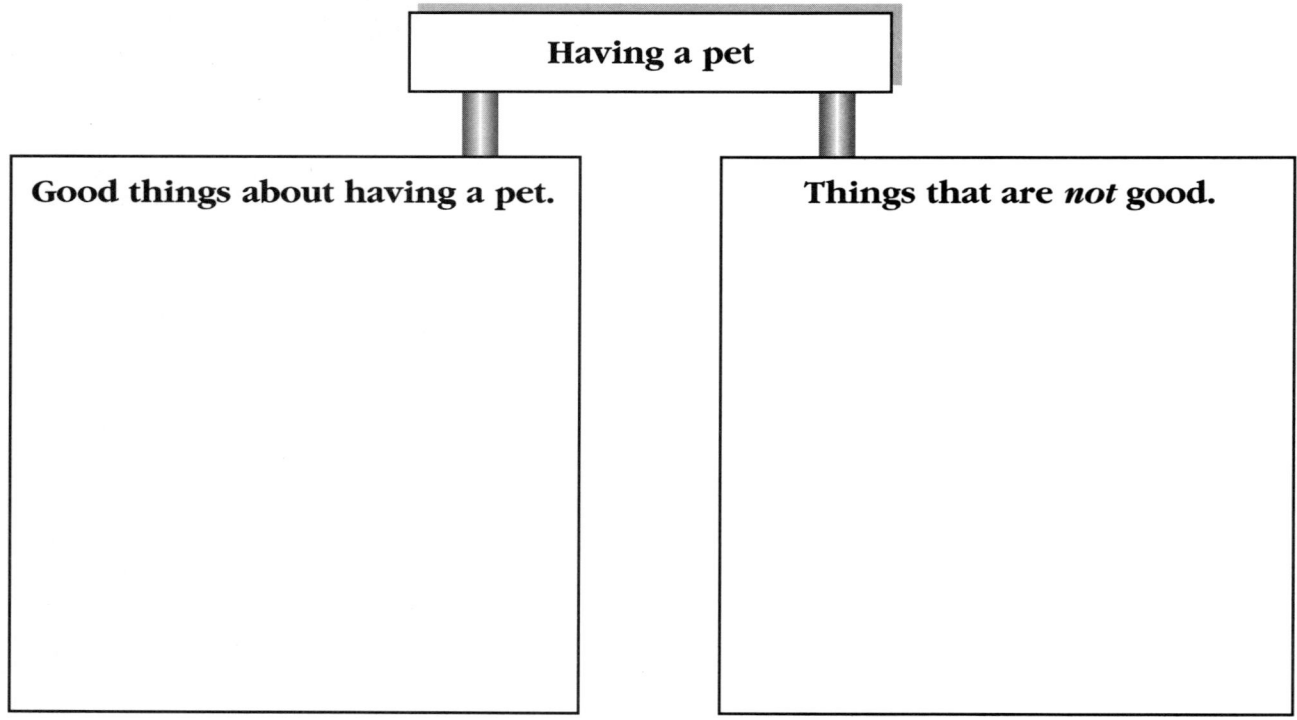

Having a pet

Good things about having a pet.

Things that are *not* good.

Go on ➤

3. In "Belling the Cat" the mice talk. Think about some TV shows and movies in which animals speak. Pick one TV show or movie. Tell what happened. Then explain why you liked or did not like the show. Be sure to give the name of the show you picked.

_____

_____

_____

_____

_____

_____

_____

_____

4. Suppose you could be any animal in the world for a day. What animal would you want to be? Tell why.

If I could be any animal in the world, I would be _____

_____

_____

_____

_____

A Zoo of Fish

There are many kinds of fish. They all live in water. But some fish live in rivers or lakes. Other fish live only in the deep ocean.

Some fish are tiny. You can hold many of them in your hand. Other fish are very big. One fish is very, very big. It is as heavy as three elephants! This fish is called the whale shark. You can probably guess why.

All fish swim. But do you know that some can fly? They are called flying fish. How does a fish "fly"? A flying fish moves its tail very quickly. This pushes the fish up out of the water. The fish goes high into the air. It looks as if it is flying. Then it drops back into the water.

Flying fish often swim together. Sometimes they "fly" at the same time. That is beautiful to see.

In the United States, flying fish live in the waters near California. These fish are very big. They are nearly two feet long. They are the biggest flying fish of all.

Now you know that some fish can "fly." But do you know that some fish can walk? It's true. One of these fish is called the mudskipper.

For additional exercises and a story about fish, see "The Long Sleep" in *More Travels* in *Goodman's Five-Star Stories,* Level A.

The mudskipper is found in Africa. It lives in muddy ponds. The mudskipper waits until the water is low. Then it jumps up onto the land. It hops around like a frog.

The mudskipper looks like a frog too. The mudskipper is brown. It has very large brown eyes. They seem to pop out of its head.

Why does the mudskipper hop onto land? It is searching for bugs. It finds bugs and eats them. Then it goes back into the water.

Some fish have very sharp teeth. One of these fish is called the piranha. A piranha's teeth are sharper than nails!

Piranhas swim in large groups. These groups are called schools. A school of piranhas can eat a large animal. They can even eat a horse in less than a minute!

You should not swim where there are piranhas. Piranhas can eat people. But this does not happen often. Piranhas do not attack all the time. They only attack when there is blood in the water. The smell of blood makes piranhas hungry.

In South America, people sometimes swim in water with piranhas. The people are safe. They make sure there is no blood in the water.

Some fish are called eels. Eels are long and thin. They do not even look like fish. Eels look like snakes. Most eels are less than three feet long. But some eels are about nine feet long.

One kind of eel is called the glass eel. Can you guess why? You can see through this eel!

A baby glass eel looks like a little leaf. When it grows up, it becomes long and thin. It looks like other eels. But you can still see through it!

The sea horse does not look like any other fish. It has a long face that looks like a horse's head. That is how the sea horse got its name. Of course, you cannot ride this sea horse. It is very small. It is smaller than a pencil.

The sea horse swims in a very strange way. Most fish swim headfirst. Not the sea horse. It swims standing straight up!

Another fish is named for a cow. It is called the cowfish. The cowfish is not big. It is not white, brown, or black. It is yellow and small. It does not moo like a cow. It does not have big eyes like a cow. Why is it called a cowfish? It has two horns on the top of its head!

Some fish look like frogs. Others look like snakes. Some fish look like horses. Other fish look like cows. Put them together in one place. What would you have? You would not have a school of fish. You would have a *zoo* of fish!

Go on ➤

I. Reading Skills

Fill in the circle next to the right answer.

1. This story is mostly about
   Ⓐ different kinds of fish.
   Ⓑ flying fish.
   Ⓒ piranhas.
   Ⓓ eels.

2. Which words belong in Box 1?
   Ⓐ can "fly" through the air
   Ⓑ has very small eyes
   Ⓒ eats bugs
   Ⓓ cannot live on land

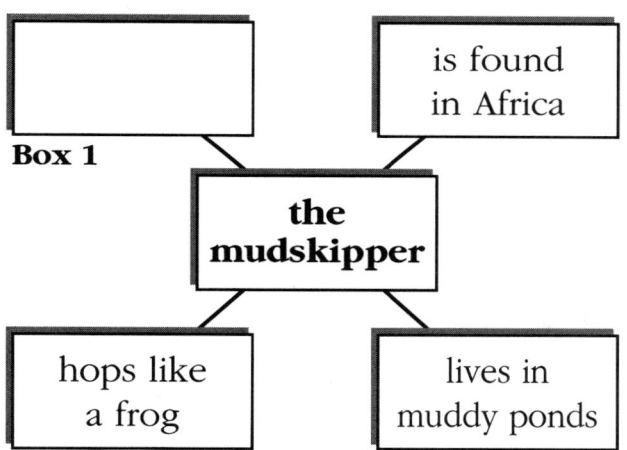

Box 1

is found in Africa

the mudskipper

hops like a frog

lives in muddy ponds

3. What is true of piranhas?
   Ⓐ They have very sharp teeth.
   Ⓑ They swim alone all the time.
   Ⓒ They cannot eat large animals.
   Ⓓ They always stay away from people.

4. The cowfish gets its name because it
   Ⓐ is very big.
   Ⓑ has horns on its head.
   Ⓒ is brown and white.
   Ⓓ has large eyes like a cow's eyes.

5. If a fish is very long and thin, it is probably
   Ⓐ a whale shark.
   Ⓑ a mudskipper.
   Ⓒ an eel.
   Ⓓ a sea horse.

Answers			
1. Ⓐ	Ⓑ	Ⓒ	Ⓓ
2. Ⓐ	Ⓑ	Ⓒ	Ⓓ
3. Ⓐ	Ⓑ	Ⓒ	Ⓓ
4. Ⓐ	Ⓑ	Ⓒ	Ⓓ
5. Ⓐ	Ⓑ	Ⓒ	Ⓓ

Go on ➤

6. The story says that some fish
   Ⓐ are not able to swim.
   Ⓑ cannot live in water.
   Ⓒ live for just a few days.
   Ⓓ look like other animals.

7. "A Zoo of Fish" shows that
   Ⓐ all fish are small.
   Ⓑ most fish are big.
   Ⓒ some fish do surprising things.
   Ⓓ most fish live in zoos.

8. Some fish are so tiny that you can hold many of them in your hand. The word *tiny* means
   Ⓐ pretty.
   Ⓑ friendly.
   Ⓒ quiet.
   Ⓓ small.

9. The mudskipper searches for food to eat. The word *searches* means
   Ⓐ looks for.
   Ⓑ needs.
   Ⓒ swims.
   Ⓓ likes.

10. Piranhas use their teeth to attack other animals. The word *attack* means
   Ⓐ help.
   Ⓑ fight.
   Ⓒ join.
   Ⓓ leave.

Answers

6.	Ⓐ	Ⓑ	Ⓒ	Ⓓ
7.	Ⓐ	Ⓑ	Ⓒ	Ⓓ
8.	Ⓐ	Ⓑ	Ⓒ	Ⓓ
9.	Ⓐ	Ⓑ	Ⓒ	Ⓓ
10.	Ⓐ	Ⓑ	Ⓒ	Ⓓ

How many questions did you get right? Circle your score below. Then fill in your **Reading Skills** score on the **Test-Taker Score Chart** on the inside of the back cover.

Number Correct	1	2	3	4	5	6	7	8	9	10
My Score	10	20	30	40	50	60	70	80	90	100

Go on ➤

II. Mechanics (capital letters, punctuation, commas, spelling, and grammar)

Fill in the circle next to the right answer.

1. Which sentence needs a capital letter?

   Ⓐ Some fish can live only in the deep ocean.

   Ⓑ The Park Street Zoo has many interesting animals.

   Ⓒ We are planning to visit the zoo in august.

2. Which sentence is not punctuated correctly?

   Ⓐ A piranha's teeth are sharp.

   Ⓑ You can find fish in rivers lakes and ponds.

   Ⓒ Have you ever seen a cowfish?

3. Which sentence needs a comma or does not use the comma correctly?

   Ⓐ My friend, Kim, has fish as pets.

   Ⓑ Some eels are nine feet long, but most eels are smaller.

   Ⓒ The piranha, a small fish has many teeth.

4. Which sentence has a word that is spelled wrong? Look at the **underlined** words.

   Ⓐ The <u>biggest</u> flying fish are found in the United States.

   Ⓑ I will be <u>stoping</u> at the pet store later.

   Ⓒ My pet fish are <u>getting</u> larger.

5. Which sentence has a mistake in grammar?

   Ⓐ Mudskippers has brown eyes.

   Ⓑ Eels are long and thin.

   Ⓒ Frogs have very strong legs.

Answers

1.	Ⓐ	Ⓑ	Ⓒ	Ⓓ
2.	Ⓐ	Ⓑ	Ⓒ	Ⓓ
3.	Ⓐ	Ⓑ	Ⓒ	Ⓓ
4.	Ⓐ	Ⓑ	Ⓒ	Ⓓ
5.	Ⓐ	Ⓑ	Ⓒ	Ⓓ

How many questions did you get right? Circle your score below. Then fill in your **Mechanics** score on the **Test-Taker Score Chart** on the inside of the back cover.

Number Correct	1	2	3	4	5
Your Score	20	40	60	80	100

Go on ➤

III. Writing

Answer the questions. You may look back at the
story as often as you wish.

1. Write one fact (something that is true) about each of
   the fish listed below.

   a. The whale shark _____

   _____

   b. The flying fish _____

   _____

   c. The mudskipper _____

   _____

   d. The piranha _____

   _____

   e. The glass eel _____

   _____

   f. The sea horse _____

   _____

   g. The cowfish _____

   _____

Go on ➤

2. Write the beginning of a short story called "I Meet a
   Piranha." Use each of the words in the box in your
   story.

swim	suddenly	afraid	down
called	boat	lucky	never

I Meet a Piranha

_____

_____

_____

_____

_____

_____

_____

_____

_____

_____

_____

_____

_____

_____

Stop